IPHONE

8/8 plus

USER GUIDE

FOR **SENIORS**

Updated iPhone 8 manual for beginners and seniors

Stephen W. Rock

Dedicated to all my readers

Acknowledgement

Ii want to say a very big thank you to Michael Lime, a 3D builder, my colleague. He gave me moral support throughout the process of writing this book.

Table of Contents

Introduction

The title of this book already gives a hint on what the book is about. It is a guide for new users of the iPhone 8/8 plus.

Dividing the whole book into three parts, the first part introduces you on how to get started with the iPhone 8/8 pus, the middle exposes a comprehensive list of tricks and how to execute them, while the last part culminates with useful maintenance tips, including troubleshooting.

Also, with the comprehensive list of commands, you'll definitely learn to be a pro in using Siri, Apple's voice assistant. You'll be a pro in using Apple Pay. You'll be an iOS 12 pro. Yes, an iOS 12 pro.

Now, start savoring the content of this book.

Chapter 1

Differences Between The iPhone 8 And The iPhone 8 Plus

IPhone 8

Released in September 2017, the iPhone 8 is said to be a bit bigger in size than the iPhone before it. But the difference is not as much as an experiment showed that the cases for iPhone 7 fit flawlessly.

The iPhone 8 is also said to be cased with glass at the back. This glass gives the phone about 10 grams extra weight. But we've got word that it is the most resilient glass ever. Except for the glass cover, iPhone 8 is said to have a dated design. Not much difference from the older iPhones in terms of look.

As with the screen, the bezel at the side of the display is a little bigger than the trending apple phones and it features an LCD display rather than a OLED. With the numbers, the phone reaches 5.45 x 2.65 and a screen of 4.7 inch. With a resolution of 1334 x 750 pixels.

One feature worth talking about also is the ability to enable true tone. With true tone, the screen is designed to switch look according to the lighting of the surroundings. What this does is that it makes the phones colors stay consistent. This screen of the iPhone 8 is said to be one of the best LCD displays around

The sound of the phone too is a lot better. It is said to be louder than the previous iPhone 7 with about 25%. The bass is a bit more and the overall sound of the phone is great.

While the outlook of phone at first glance might not look any different from previous models, it does pack more advanced features. Like for example, the Bionic processor is A11 chip and that makes the performance a lot faster.

Now with the camera, iPhone 8 is equipped with a f/1.8 12 megapixel camera for the back. This is capable of up to 5x zoom. The rear camera is able to shoot 4K videos at up to 60 fps. It is also capable of shooting 240fps (frames per second) for slow-mo

At the front, we have the 7 megapixel FaceTime camera that uses f/2.2 aperture and BSI sensor. There's also the option for Slow-Sync Flash. This makes lowlight photos look amazing.

As regard the battery, this one's kind of low. It's has a battery of 1821mAh. Should last you a day if used carefully. The iPhone 8 identifies with a 2GB RAM and a storage of 64GB or 256 GB

iPhone 8 Plus

iPhone 8 Plus signifies the last of the iPhones with a home button. Though we don't know what can happen In the future. But I think Apple is pretty much done with the homebutton. And even though the recent iPhone X series is the talk of town, Apple still has the iPhone 8 Plus for sale.

This phone still carries the same design as the iPhone 8 except for two basic things.

First of all the most obvious; The size. The size of the iPhone 8 Plus is 6.24 x 3.07 inches. And it features a screen of 5.5 inches. An improvement from the little brother featuring just 4.7 inches. And with big screens you should expect sharper displays. And yes it does. It comes with a display resolution of 1920 x 1080.

So with an iPhone 8 Plus, you get higher quality display than iPhone 8's 1334 x 750. It's only in the iPhone X that we see Apple moving over to OLED displays, The iPhone 8 Plus still features a LCD display. And the iPhone 8 has a PPI of only 326, the iPhone 8 Plus features a 401 PPI.

In the area of performance however, there's not much difference. Like for example they both have a Bionic chipset of A11 that's equipped with HexaCore. The RAM for iPhone 8 is 2GB while iPhone 8 Plus features higher with a storage space of up to 3GB. But that shouldn't mean a lot as RAM comes into play when you're multitasking, so unless you're a multitask guru, the extra 1GB shouldn't mean a lot.

Now the second basic difference is the camera. One features only one rear camera, the other has two. And as you've guessed it, iPhone 8 Plus slides in with double cameras. The double camera features 12 megapixels but one of them is capable of shooting with an aperture of f/1.8 wide angle lens and the other camera with f/2.8. Both with Telephoto and Optical Image Stabilization.

On the front however they're both equal as they both give a 7 megapixel sensor with f/2.2 aperture.

Still on the camera, the Plus offers an option for Portrait mode while the other does not. With Portrait mode, you be able to shoot remarkable photos and make the backgrounds blurred and add bokeh to spice up the image. Use portrait mode for all your images and you take your photo experience to a whole new level.

Chapter 2

Secure Your iPhone With Face ID

Setting up Face ID

Before we set anything up, let's make sure there's nothing blocking your face or the phones TrueDepth camera. Try to keep the phone with arms length. And don't worry about contacts or glasses, Face ID can work with them.

To set it up,

1. Go to **Settings**
2. Choose **Face ID and Passcode**. Enter your passcode.
3. Select **Set up Face ID**
4. Put your phone in front of your face and hit **Get started**.

5. Make sure your face is in the frame. Move your head gently to complete the circle. When it's done, hit **Continue.**

6. You'll be asked to do it a second time. Do the same thing and click **Done**.

Using the Face ID

Tap to wake or raise to wake your phone. Hold it in portrait orientation and it should scan your face.
If you're in bright sunlight, you might want to bring the camera closer to your face.

Face ID has been tested to unlock even when you're wearing sunglasses, but not all. So if you're trying to unlock your phone but it isn't recognizing, pull the sunglass off.

How To Charge iPhone Wirelessly.

Later versions of iPhone (iPhone 8 and higher) have a glass back that enables Qi certified chargers to charge the phone wirelessly. There are many Qi certified chargers. But there are two which are Apple certified; Mophie and Belkin.

Charging wirelessly

To charge wirelessly, what you want to do is;

1. Plug your charger to the power. Be sure to use a power adapter that's recommended by the manufacturer.
2. Make sure to put your charger on a flat surface
3. Lay your iPhone in the middle of the charger with its screen facing upwards and your phone should start charging

That not all. Here are a few things to make to wireless charging run smoothly

- If vibration is turned on, your phone might very well move its position when it gets a notification as you're charging. Try to turn off vibration, at least when you charge

- Make sure your phone isn't connected to a USB when you're charging wirelessly, it won't charge.
- If your iPhone has a thick or magnetic case, remove it before charging. It might charge slowly or not at all.
- When charging, your phone might get somewhat hot. When it does, move it to a cooler environment.

Chapter 3

iPhone 8/8 Plus Tips And Tricks

Video quality like never before

Talking about video quality, iPhone 8 and 8 Plus are able to shoot rally high quality videos. You know how 1080p resolution took the world by a storm? Yeah, iPhone 8 gives you 4 times that.

That's right. They call it 4k resolution. Just imagine how sharp and vivid 4k can be. With iPhone 8 and 8 Plus you can shoot 4k at 60 frames per second.

Using 4k is actually simple, just;
1. Go to **Settings**
2. Enter **Camera**
3. Select **Record video**
4. Select **4k at 60 fps** from the options it shows

I just want you note something. When you shoot with such massive value and quality, of course the size is not going to be 20KB. It's definitely going to be heavy. And since Apple does not provide a slot for microSD, you might want to go for the option of 256GB if you know you'll be shooting more videos

Don't stop shooting

Do you remember that time when you were shooting a video and then your eyes catches an interesting image, you want to take a photo of it but you can't. You're shooting a video.

When that scenario happens with older phones, then only thing you can do is sit and watch as the awesome image goes away. But that shouldn't happen again. I mean, you have your iPhone 8. Just take the photo already.

With your iPhone 8, you can take a picture while shooting a video. Just
1. Enter **Camera**
2. Swipe over to **Video**
3. Start shooting the video
4. Look for a white circle at the corner of the screen and tap it.
5. The picture is taken and saved in **Gallery**

There's a But, though. If you take photo while shooting, you don't get the full quality as a normal camera picture.

While the snap as you shoot gets up to 3840 x 2160, the normal camera can be as clear as 4032 x 3024. But at least it's something.

Impressive format for both photo and video

We just talked about the rate at which the 4k resolution can swallow up the space of your iPhone. Yes it does but it would have been much worse if it wasn't for the new format for video and photo in the iPhone 8 and iPhone 8 Plus.

The formats are HEVC and HEIF. Standing for High Efficiency Video Coding and High Efficiency Image File respectively, what they both do is that they still allows you to take you video and photo at the same high quality but takes up smaller spaces

To start to save more space,
1. Enter **Settings**
2. Go to **Camera**
3. Then **Format**
4. Select **High Efficiency.**

Use The True Tone

This true tone is the capability of your phone to shift and change the display of your phone depending on the lighting conditions of your surroundings. It will then display colors that are steady relating to your environment.

This sweet feature was first accessible on the iPad Pro alone, but now it's open to iPhones. And iPhone 8 has it.

To turn this on or off;
1. Enter the **Settings app**
2. Move to **Display and Brightness**
3. Turn on the toggle for **true tone**

A quicker way can be to;
1. Slide and enter the **Control Center**
2. You should see the brightness slider, Long press on it
3. Turn on **true tone**

Enable Auto brightness

The auto brightness can be really helpful. IT doesn't make your phones display too low or bright. When the screens too low, you can see the contents well. And when it's to bright, it can suck away battery pretty fast.

But everyone is different some prefer to use the Auto brightness while some totally dislike it

The auto brightness has changed location on the iPhone. On the former iOS, you would have to move to Display accommodations to change Auto brightness. So if you want to turn on or off Auto brightness, here's how

1. Go to **Settings**
2. Select **Accessibility**
3. Choose **Display accommodations.**

Allow Siri know you

You know Siri, the apple assistant. Though Siri can be cold sometimes, it can be a very helpful depending on how you set it. If you let Siri to know you are, if can be able to reconnect you back to your phone in case you lose it.

That's like a Life Saver, at least your investment you have to go to waste when you lose it.

To tell Siri who you are, you have to verify that you have added yourself as a contact. After that, all you do is
1. Enter **Settings**
2. Select **Siri and Search**
3. Then **My information**

Then from the contacts you can choose your own name.

Setting Custom Ringtones

This one's a lovely feature. It enables you find out who is calling you without looking at your phone's display. How this works is that you put a particular ringtone for each person.

When Justin Bieber's tone start playing, you know it's Mark that's calling. Or if you start hearing Celine Dion's track, that'll notify you that special one is calling. It depends on if you set it like that though.

1. Go to **Contacts**
2. Choose the contacts you wish to put a ring tone for.
3. Scroll down and click **Ringtone**
4. Pick the tone you want
5. If you want to add a custom vibration, Hit **Vibration** and chose your desired vibration
6. To create your own vibration, just scroll down to the bottom.

Customize Ringtone in your iPhone 8 and iPhone 8 Plus.

Just as you're able to customize and edit so many things on your iPhone 8 and Plus, you have the ability to customize the way your control center shows up on your phone.

This is really helpful because you'll be able to remove the items that you don't use often and put the ones you really need. Like if you dont use much of Calculator, you can remove it and put something else, say Magnifier.

To do this;

1. Enter **Settings**
2. Choose **Control Center**.
3. Tap **Customize Controls**
4. If you remove a feature, hit the **red button** beside the control
5. If you add a Control, press the **green circle**.

Use The Live Photos

Live photos can be a lot of fun. It records a few seconds before you shoot a photo and after you shoot it. This enables you to store memorable moments. While photos tell a story, live photos take you in the story.

To do this;
1. Enter the **Camera**.
2. Put your camera in photo mode and ensure that **Live Photo** is turned on
3. Just hold your phone and don't move.
4. Take the photo

Use The Sprit Level

In your iPhone 8 and Plus, you have numerous features kept in it. Your iPhone has the hidden ability to work in a spirit level.

What the spirit level does is that it shows you how uneven or straight a surface is when you rest your iPhone on it. You wouldn't know because it's not a standalone app. You won't find something like **The Spirit Level App**. No, Apple stashed it away in a different app; the compass app.

So that means that to open the spirit level,
1. You have to open up the **Compass App**.
2. Slide left.
3. The spirit level should be revealed

Using Do Not Disturb

IPhone 8 and 8 plus are really great phones. And one of the things contributing to its greatness is the ability to switch to **Do Not Disturb**.

These days, people tend to get distracted when they drive and it's because of their phones. Most of the times, it's usually not their fault. They are determined not to press their phones while they drive. But then as soon as they zoom off they get a notification and they feel tempted to read it.

You can avoid that temptation by using your iPhone to the full. Use the setting called **Do not disturb**. Once you enable it, it'll silence notifications and calls.

Want to try this?
1. Head over to the **Setting**
2. Choose **Do Not Disturb**
3. You should see tree options, **Manually, Automatically, When connected to Car Bluetooth**.

When connected to Car Bluetooth can be great cause as soon as you hook up your phone to the Bluetooth, it'll switch to **Do not disturb** mode. **Automatically** might not be the right choice. Your phone may end up switching to Do not disturb if you're in the train because it determines whether you're the one driving or not by means of motion and movement.

Switch To Low Power Mode.

Just as we said, Auto brightness can help your phone not to eat much battery, but there's also another feature that does more than that. It's the **Low Power Mode** option.

If you're one who uses the phone for a long time without charging, this will really come in handy. Low Power Mode switches off the items in your iPhone that sucks battery.

Of course it'll lower the brightness. The screen also goes dark more quickly. Hey Siri is gone. Background app refresh is gone, Mail fetch gone.

All of this is to save power.
1. Enter **Settings**
2. Tap **Battery**
3. Choose **Low Power Mode**

To even make it easier, you don't have to travel to Settings. You can just add it to the control center. That is after you add it yourself

1. Move to **Settings**
2. Then **Control center**

3. Select **Customize Controls**.
4. Tap the green button next to **Low Power Mode**

Start Dragging And Dropping

It's no lie that dragging and dropping for apple devices were only limited to iPads. But on the iPhone 8 and Plus, you now have the power to use the drag and drop. You also have the ability to do the multi-drag option.

As the name multi-drag connotes, this is the ability for the phone to drag several applications and drop in another screen or anywhere else.

To enable this,
1. Long press on the app you want to move. If you want to move multiple, press those apps too.
2. Now drag and drop it in the place you wish
3. Don't release your hand just yet. Wait a few seconds.
4. If you drag and drop in a app, there will be folder created for the two apps

Embrace Slow Sync

If you're a photography guru, then you should have no problem understanding what Slow Sync Flash means. That's what high end cameras do. But as for we normal humans that don't use cameras every day, we can be kind of oblivious to what Slow Sync Flash is.

Slow Sync Flash is the ability of you phone to shoot at a slower shutter speed while shining the flash quickly. Most phones today shoot at a high shutter speed. And that's not a problem in bright lighting.

But when it comes to low lighting you don't want to shoot with your flash using fast shutter speed. The photo won't turn out very nice.

But with your iPhone 8 and 8 Plus you have the power of slow sync flash to use in the dark. The result; A beautiful image.

To use Slow Sync Flash, all you just need to do is use the flash to shoot.

iPhone 8's Wireless Charging

iPhone 8 and 8 Plus, the amazing phones in their glory are equipped with wireless charging. This makes way for a charging experience that's easy and effective. No more having to carry around charging cords to charge to your phone.

This is made possible because of the back of the iPhone 8 an 8 Plus which is made up of glass. This glass back uses QI certified chargers to charge the iPhone wirelessly. You can see QI certified chargers easily in stores. Especially the approved ones; Belkin and Mophie. Even Apples Airpower is underway.

To charge you phone wirelessly, just plug the charger to power then you put your iPhone on the pad as the screen faces upwards and your phone should start charging.

Rank Your Downloads

There will be many times when you wish you could just rank your downloads or prioritize them. Your iPhone 8 makes that possible with no hassle.

This will help you make the most of your iPhone 8 as it will really come in handy if you're downloading several apps. It will help you save time and download what you really need real quick.

To do this
1. Press and hold on the **Touch ID** button on your phone.
2. A menu will show now, select **Prioritize downloads** from the options.

Type Emoji Faster.

In this modern world, emojis are really taking over chats. Everybody loves them. They help express feelings in ways that texts can't.

But when typing, no one has the time to go to the emoji gallery and start looking for the emoji of choice. That just wastes time. But in your iPhone 8, you have the ability to input and add shortcuts for the emoji.

1. Go to **Settings**
2. Enter **General**
3. Then **Keyboards**
4. Select **Add new keyboard.**
5. Tap **Emoji**

Once you've added the emoji
1. Go to **Settings**
2. Then **General**
3. Select **Keyboard**
4. Choose **Add new Shortcut**

Form here you can put a word that will become an emoji. Like for example, you can input that when you type **omg**, the shocked emoji will appear.

Lock Camera Lens

When you're shooting a video on your iPhone, you want the best quality you can get from your phone. And you're iPhone 8 will give you that quality. But if you don't set it right, it can actually switch lenses and that may not be what you want.

You don't have you worry, with the new feature in iPhone 8, you have ability to lock the camera lenses without any problem.

1. Go to **Settings**
2. Select **Camera**
3. Then **Record video**
4. Toggle on **Lock Camera Lens**

Recording The Screen

In the past you would need third party apps to record screen activity. But with the iOS 11, you can record the screen with phone's inbuilt feature.

1. Enter the **Settings**
2. Select **Control Center**
3. Tap **Customize controls**
4. Press the **green button** beside **Screen Recording**

Wirelessly Transfer Data To Your iPhone 8

If you want to sell your previous iPhone or give to a friend or cousin, there's something you want to do first. You want to upgrade that phone to the latest iOS. This is because with the latest iOS, you have a feature that allows you move the contents on your old iPhone to the now one wirelessly.

You will just use the old iPhone to scan your new iPhone 8. And after you scan, you'll be asked to input your authentication code. After you authenticate, the two phones will be synced and the transfer of all your settings, contents, data should begin.

During this transfer process, your passwords too will be in unison. With this new method, you can say bye to backing up to iTunes and putting back to your new phone.

Using Portrait Lighting

This one's is a big feature. Though it's for the iPhone 8 Plus alone. They call it **Portrait Lighting**. With Portrait Lighting, you have various lighting styles from Contour Light to Stage Light to Studio Light to Natural light and more.

With Portrait lighting, there's no need for filters. It uses the information gotten on your face to give you the best of the different lighting selections.

To use this,
1. Open your **Camera**
2. Beside Photo, Select the **Portrait Mode**.
3. From here you should be able to see some circles on top of the shutter. Scroll through the options and choose your desired lighting effect.
4. Click Shutter

If you're using stage light or stage light mono, you should try to make sure that face fills up the circle as much as you can.

In portrait mode, if you don't want the blurry effect,

1. Go to **Photos**
2. Pick the image of the Portrait mode
3. Select **Edit**
4. You should see a yellow logo at the top, tap it
5. Once you tap it, the effect should be off.

Venture Into The World Of AR

AR short for Augmented Reality is an advancement in technology that fixes information on the phone into real life. It can put characters in a game on your couch right in your sitting room. Though it's digitally of course.

One of the games that you can dive into AR with is Pokemon Go. And as you've guessed it your iPhone 8 is capable of this feat

When you open the game and you point your camera at any object in the real world, the app will show what your camera sees. Then you can put a character that's around to the object. In the real world nothing is happening, it's on your phone that the action is taking place.

With AR, you don't need any special extra kit, or goggles. The wonders are all in your phone.

Use Auto Call

On your phone, the feature Emergency SOS is enabled by default already. But there's something that you haven't tried yet. It's the **Auto Call**. What **Auto Call** does is that it after you quickly click the power button five times it will automatically call the services for emergency.

But when you press five times, it won't start calling emergency immediately. A selection to call will first show up. **Touch ID** will become ineffective for a while. It's until after you put in your Passcode, that **Touch ID** can become available again.

To be able to use this feature,
1. Fire up the **Settings**
2. Select **Emergency SOS**
3. Turn on the toggle for **Auto Call**.
4. If you would like to be informed as you're calling the emergency, you can add a countdown sound.

Delete Text Easily

There will be times when you will type out mistakes, or you change your mind and want to clear out what you've written, or maybe autocorrects just made your message life more miserable. When that happens it's almost a guarantee that you will start holding down your backspace for centuries to erase the bulky texts.

But don't do that, you a have a breathtaking phone now, remember? All you do is just shake your iPhone 8 and you see an option to Undo Typing. Select that and you are able to clear all in a split second.

Okay let's say you cleared everything but then you suddenly remember that there are some important words and ideas that you want to bring back. Just do the same, shake again and select Redo.

Check Out Where You Been.

Maybe because of curiosity you want to find out what your phone usually tracks so that you will see options of locations. Or you want to find out your most visited places.

All you can do is
1. Move to **Settings**.
2. Enter **Privacy**
3. Select **Location Services**
4. Then **System services**
5. Choose **Significant Locations** or **Frequent Locations**

From here you can see the places you visit the most. IF you don't want this again, you can just turn off

Scanning Documents

You don't have to use third party apps to do this. You can do it right on your iPhone 8 with no hassle.

All you do is;
1. Enter **Notes App**
2. Make a **New note**
3. If keyboard is shown, click the **plus** button at the top of the keyboard. If keyboard is not open, look the **plus** button at the bottom of the display
4. Select **Scan Documents**
5. For an enriched scan, click the overflow icon and choose between color, grayscale or black and white

Chapter 4

How To Use Apple Pay

It is now ever easy to use Apple pay. It can even be done through the iMessage app. All you do to activate is place the top of your phone near the **NFC** card terminal while putting your finger on the iPhone's sensor for Touch ID. But to be able to perform all these wonders, you've got set Apple pay up first.

Setting Up The Apple Pay

1. Open **Wallet**
2. Select **Add Credit or Debit card**.
3. Put your card details. Your card will now be verified with your bank
4. Once that is done, you are able to use Apple Pay.

Using The Apple Pay.

1. Put your phone near the card reader and what will appear on the screen should be the image of your card.
2. If you use Touch ID, Place your finger on the Touch ID sensor. Once your fingerprint is confirmed, you're golden.

If you want another card, press the one that is on the screen and select a different card. Real simple, uh?

However if your phone uses Face ID like iPhone X and higher, the process is a little different. It's not hard though. You just click twice on the side button. Then put your face to the camera so it can scan your face. After this, you simply hold the phone toward the card reader. Double click the side button again, if you want to use another card and just select a different card.

Chapter 5

Tips for using iOS 12 effectively

Saving Your Passwords

In the iOS 12 there a totally cool feature that helps users be able to follow up on their passwords. The new iOS is armed with a feature called **AutoFill Passwords**. This is usually kept in the iCloud keychain.

With this, you can add your own username and passwords from your **Settings app** to set for only some apps and websites. This feature will fill in your information automatically for you once you use Face ID or Touch ID after it identifies the ones that are logged

Ability To Turn On 'Do Not Disturb' During Bedtime.

The **Do Not Disturb** option got totally revamped in the iOS 12. With its extra feature, you are able to customize it more to suit your taste. Not only can you state clearly what times you want **Do Not Disturb** to be on at day, you can even set it to Bedtime mode.

If you set it, this will quiet down all the notifications all the way till the morning. To let you know that it the feature is set, the screen will display just the date and time and become dim.

Measuring Objects With An App.

Using the camera of your iPhone, iOS 12 allows you to measure objects with AR. When you use the measure app, you'll be able to measure different objects.

All you do is,

1. Open the **Measure app**.
2. Fix your iPhone's camera on the object to measure
3. Follow the guides it gives to line up your phone correctly.
4. Next, to view the measurements, you just click the display

Every display will always show the option to switch form inches to centimeters. Of course it doesn't give an accurate measurement like a hardware tape rule, it is really handy if you just want to take a quick measurement of an item.

Insert Siri shortcuts

There's a new advancement with Siri in the iOS 12. It's the option to add immediate actions and shortcut to Siri. Thought this option is still in beta for now and you can't do plenty with it, there are still some perks you can enjoy.

Like how you can set a voice commands so that Siri can do some specific tasks. Example, **View New photos.**
If you want to set a voice command'
1. Enter your **Settings**.
2. Selects **Siri and Search**
3. Click **My Shortcuts**

Once that is open you will be able select anyone that Siri suggests.

Track your screen time

In the iOS 12, apple is trying to urge us to use our phones lesser so we can have time for other important activities. There's this new feature, **Screen time**.

Screen time is an opportunity for you to set Downtime, check your phone usage and find out which apps are really eating away your time. When you use down time, you are able to put away your phone by restraining some applications from forwarding notifications.

Place Limits on apps

This is also one of the perks of screen time. It enables you to set app limits. This will enable you to reduce the time you spend on certain apps. You will be able to set how long the ban should last and for which days.

If you want to set app limits.
1. Fire up the **Settings app**
2. Move to **Screen time**
3. Then **App limits**. Select the groups of apps you want to set limit. Click the **Add**

Easy Force Closing apps.

With the iOS 12, the process of force closing apps is a lot simpler. Not only simpler also quicker. All you do is swipe up from the bottom of the display and just start swiping the apps you want to quit like that.

Y'know, previously force closing apps on phones without home button on previous iOS will have to take a longer method. You'll have to swipe up and hold down and wait before a minus sign will appear, then you now click

But now with newer phones like the iPhone XS and XS Max, they all have the iOS 12, so the process is a lot simpler.

Chapter 6

How To Use Siri On Your Iphone

Siri is the ever helpful apple voice assistant that you dish out commands to on your iPhone and it just it just carries it out for you.

But something to note is that there's not a specific app icon for Siri that you just tap and it open. So how then do you access Siri. For newer generations of iPhones, accessing Siri can be a little confusing even if you have been using previous versions of iPhone. All of that we will cover here

How to invoke Siri

By Clicking the home button or side button

On older versions of iPhone, pressing and holing the home button on your device will call up Siri. But on the iPhone X and higher, you summon Siri by pressing the button at the side of the phone.

By using the Bluetooth headset button.

If you use a headset that has remote, press and hold the button at the center and you should hear a ding.

By saying hey Siri

If your iPhone is iOS 8 or higher, you can summon Siri hands free by saying 'Hey Siri'. But you've got to first set it up.

1. Got to **Settings**
2. Choose **Siri & Search**
3. Enable **Listen For** 'Hey Siri' and obey the prompts it provides
4. From now you can summon Siri without having to press anything just say **"Hey Siri"**

What Can Siri do for you,

- Send messages for you
- Set a timer for you
- Play music
- Send tweets
- Check the weather
- Schedule events
- Send emails

- Calculate
- Find locations

Here are some things you can ask Siri

- 'Hey Siri, Set an alarm for 6 am'
- 'Hey Siri, What is the time New York?'
- 'Hey Siri, schedule a meeting with Sarah for Tuesday at 11oclock
- 'Hey Siri, how cold will it be today?'
- 'Hey Siri, remind me to do the dishes?'
- 'Hey Siri, play me Roar by Katy Perry'
- 'Hey Siri, call David Randall
- 'Hey Siri, open the Settings App'
- 'Hey Siri, how do I say hello in Spanish?'
- 'Hey Siri, who is the President of Iceland?'
- 'Hey Siri, turn off Bluetooth'

How to type and ask Siri

If you're the type that doesn't really fancy talking to Siri, you don't have to say something. You can just type your command. Though you'll have to set it up first

Here's how.

1. Enter **Settings**
2. Go to **General**
3. Select **Accessibility**
4. Move down to Siri and click the line
5. Switch on **Type To Siri**
6. The next time you activate Siri, all you do is type in your command

Tips To Ensure That Siri Serves You Well

While the apples virtual assistant is known for its top notch abilities, you may encounter some problems with it. Implement these few tips to allow Siri to better

Control how long Siri will listen

You have the power to control how long Siri will continue to encode your commands. You don't have to wait for it to recognize that you have stopped talking.

Just make sure that while you're asking your question or saying your command, you're holding down the power button

Alter Siri's language.

One of the key reasons why Siri may not understand your commands well can be because of your language. Even in English. Let's say you speak UK English. Siri may misinterpret your commands. So what you want to do is set the English to 'English (United Kingdom)

To adjust the language,
1. Enter the **Settings**
2. Go to **Siri and Search**
3. Select Language
4. Choose your desired language.

Having Smooth Data Connection

If you don't have data connection, Siri won't work. How Siri functions is that it records your voice and sends it to a server which converts your sayings and gives it back as text.

So if you're not connected to the internet, Siri is not going to work.

Changing Siri's gender

If you're a male and you prefer to have a male virtual brother around, you can switch the gender. Same goes for females.

Just,

1. Enter **Settings**
2. Then **Siri and Search**
3. Choose **Siri Voice**
4. Select your preferred voice.

Chapter 7

How To Maintain Your iPhone

We all know that iPhones are not biscuit change. They cost high. Well, they give superb quality so they are very well worth it. But such an investment will go to total waste if you don't take proper care of your treasure.

So here are some iOS maintenance tips for your consumption.

Put The Unwanted In The Garbage Truck

Do you remember that game that your buddy told you to try out and you felt it was total trash? Or yes, that app your neighbor introduced to you only for to find that it was a complete waste of time. Yes those applications. I'm pretty sure they are still sitting there in you app list

Throw them out and send them packing immediately. Not only do they use up the space of the phone, they also make it sluggish and your device slow. To delete an app, press and hold the app until it shakes like it's waving 'hey look at me' and delete or press the X at the corner.

Back Them Up

It's funny how many people do the bad stuff and only few do the good, like backing up your iPhones. You need to train yourself so that it becomes a habit.

Reason why backing up is so essential is because of this. Let's say your iPhone gets missing (I really hope that doesn't happen) or you there was a software update gone wrong or your device becomes faulty, retrieving your files will be almost impossible.

So don't wait for me, just back your phone up. You can back your phone up with iCloud or iTunes. In fact what's stopping you, just do both!

Update iOS

You be like 'Who needs an update. My iOS is just fine'. And I want you discard that feeling and throw it far away.

You need an update. With every new iOS there are fixes to bugs, updates for security, and brand new features and perks. You stick to your old iOS and it will be like you're living in the Stone Age.

What more, updating is like the easiest thing to do. Since we have OTA (Over The Air), updating iOS is just a matter of minutes.

To update,
1. Make sure to back up your phone as we warned earlier
2. Enter **Settings**
3. Then **General**
4. Then Choose **Software update**.
5. If an update is available, click **Download and install**.

Phone case and Screen protector

We all know how phone cases and screen protectors saves our lives every once in a while. Okay, not our life per say, it's our phones. Whenever your phone drops, a protective phone case will help to absorb the effect and shock of the fall.

And screens, oh screens are really special. And believe me when I say that you do not want them to break. So just buy a screen protector.

When you're purchasing either of the two, make sure it's of good quality and the design is what you desire.

Chapter 8

Prolonging Your iPhones Battery Life.

As with maintenance of phones, we all know how much battery means to us. Check out these tips to extend your phones battery life.

Forget Quitting Apps

You may probably be doing this, quitting apps regularly, I usually do so too in the past. But stop. you might think that you're saving you're battery, but actually you're degrading it.

In 2014, Apple explained to us that quitting apps sucks more battery as the next time you want to open the app, it will start all over again thereby, eating the batter.

Using The Auto Brightness Option.

Using full screen brightness sucks away your battery and I'm sure you know that. Unless you really need the extra brightness, don't be stubborn just use auto brightness.

This adjusts the screens brightness to the surroundings you're in.

Turn Low Power Mode On

Normally when you're phone reaches 20%, you'll be prompted to switch to low power mode. But you don't have to wait for your phone to urge you before you switch it. You can do it right after you finishing charging.

Low power mode stops all the background tasks and gives you more battery.

Turn Off Bluetooth.

It's not a new thing that putting your Bluetooth on regularly reduces the battery life. So if you're not using the Bluetooth, just put it off

Disclaimer

In as much as the author believes beginners will find this book helpful in learning how to use the iPhone 8/8 plus, it is only a small book. It should not be relied upon solely for all iPhone tricks and troubleshooting.

About the author

Stephen Rock has been a certified apps developer and tech researcher for more than 12 years. Some of his 'how to' guides have appeared in a handful of international journals and tech blogs. He loves rabbits.

Facebook page @ Techgist